All About...

Cats and Kittens

Fun facts and tips about your pets

SCHOLASTIC

Contents

Each year, thousands of unwanted cats and kittens are re-homed by the RSPCA.

This book has been created to help you to give your pet cat or kitten a happy, healthy life.
Read on and find out all about cats and kittens.

Quick quiz

So you think you know all about cats and kittens? Take this true or false quiz to see if you've got what it takes to be a responsible owner:

1 Cats have been kept as pets since Victorian times.

2 Tabby cats have an 'M' mark in the fur on their forehead.

3 Cats can make three sounds: purring, meowing and growling.

4 Cats spend up to two-thirds of their time asleep.

5 The average cat lives for seven years.

Answers

1 False. Turn to page 20-25 to find out more about cats in history. **2** True. **3** False. Turn to page 48 to find out the truth. **4** True. Turn to page 73 to find out more about sleep. **5** False. Find out more about their life-span on page 81.

Meet the cat family

Cats are sleek, slinky animals with fur coats, sharp claws and sharp teeth. Their bodies are built for hunting, especially at night. But cats don't just mean your pet moggy, snoozing on your lap. The cat family also includes your kitty's wild cousins – 'big cat' species, which include lions, tigers, jaguars and leopards as well as cheetahs, lynxes, pumas, bobcats and ocelots.

Did you know?

A group of pet cats is called a 'clowder'.
A group of kittens is called a 'kindle'.

The top four fang-tastic first cat facts

1 The earliest cat cousins might have been weasel-like creatures with long legs. They probably lived in tropical forests around 50 million years ago.

2 The fiercest first cats were sabre-toothed tigers. As big as lions, they had vicious, curved teeth as long as this page. They use these fearsome fangs for stabbing bison and mammoths to eat.

3 Thousands of sabre-tooth tiger fossils were found in a tar pit in the USA. The cats came to hunt other animals that had got trapped in the tar, then also got stuck fast.

4 Around 13,000 years ago, supersized lions roamed Britain. They weighed as much as small cars and had long legs for chasing after giant deer and woolly mammoths.

Kitty cousins

Lions, tigers, jaguars and leopards are the largest of the 'big cats'. They are all big, lean powerful hunting machines. Here a quick spotter's guide to the fab four...

Lion

Lives in: Africa and India

Weighs: up to 272 kg

Diet includes:
Zebra, antelope, buffalo

Tiger

Lives in: India, China,
South East Asia, Russia

Weighs: up to 300 kg

Diet includes:
Deer, wild boar, buffalo, as well as
fish, birds and reptiles

Leopard

Lives in: Africa and South Asia

Weighs: up to 90 kg

Diet includes:
Antelope, wildebeest, monkeys
as well as fish, birds and reptiles

Jaguar

Lives in: South America

Weighs: up to 140 kg

Diet includes:
Tapir, deer, turtles, snakes, fish

Did you know?

Only the four largest species of the big cats – lions, tigers,
leopards and jaguars – can roar.
Others such as cheetahs and snow leopards cannot.

The top five BIG cat facts

5 A tiger's stripes might look showy but they're actually brilliant camouflage. They hide a tiger among the long stalks of grass so its prey can't see it coming. Every tiger's stripe pattern is unique.

4 Cheetahs can speed along as fast as cars. They have bendy backbones for leaping and sharp claws that grip the ground like the spikes in running shoes.

3 Most big cats are big loners but lions love company. They live in families called prides, made up of males, females and their cubs.

2 Leopards use trees as larders. They drag their kill high up into the branches to stop other animals eating it.

1 Pumas are known by more names than any other cat. In some areas of the United States, as well as being called cougars, they are sometimes called mountain lions, catamounts, painters, purple feathers, mountain screamers and deer tigers!

Tiger rescue

Many big cats are in serious danger...

At one time, tigers roamed across large parts of Asia. Today, there may be only a few thousand left. Their wild forest homes are being destroyed to make space for farmland and there isn't enough of their own prey left to hunt. This means they are more likely to eat farmers' animals, which angers the farmers, who sometimes shoot the tigers if they have eaten their livestock. Many tigers have been killed by poachers for their skins and other body parts.

Conservation groups, like the WWF (Worldwide Fund for Nature), are working hard to try to save tigers. They help local people understand more about tigers. They put guards in the forest to stop poachers. They move tigers that stray into villages to other forests further away.

Sadly, it may already be too late...

Lions

Lions are the second largest big cats and are sometimes called the 'king of beasts' because of their majestic looks.

Amazing lion facts

Lions have huge, curved claws that can be up to 7.5 centimetres (3 inches) long. These are used to climb, as well as to catch and hold prey.

Although lions are huge animals, they are very fast and can reach speeds of up to 56 kilometres per hour (35 miles per hour) when chasing prey.

Male lions have manes of long fur covering their heads and necks. A large mane makes a lion look more intimidating. A lion with a longer mane tends to be the leader of a group of lions, or 'pride', as lions with smaller manes are less likely to fight him.

Female lions are known as lionesses. They do most of the hunting while the male lions protect the pride. Females often work in small teams to bring down larger prey such as buffalo and wildebeest.

Did you know?

A lion's roar can be heard up to
8 kilometres (5 miles away).

The top five purr-fect pet cat facts

5 Cats are the most popular pet on the planet with more than 600 million worldwide.

4 It's thought that pet cats are descended from wild cats that live in Africa. Their posh scientific name is *Felis silvestris catus*.

3 Cats were first kept as pets about 4,000 years ago. They were used to catch mice and rats that gobbled up farmers' grain supplies.

2 But cats might have been pets for even longer. A cat's bones were found in a 9,500-year-old human grave in Cyprus. Perhaps it was buried with its owner?

1 The best mouser ever was a cat called Towser from Scotland. In her lifetime, she caught a world-record-breaking 28,899 mice, not to mention rats and rabbits.

Did you know?

Stuck for what to call your cat?
Here are some of the most
popular pet names:

- Girls...
  Poppy
  Bella
  Daisy
  Millie
  Lily

- Boys...
  Charlie
  Felix
  Alfie
  Oscar
  Jasper

21

Cats' tales

The ancient Egyptians weren't the only ones who had interesting ideas about cats. Throughout history, cats have played a big part in people's stories and beliefs.

The top five things you might not believe about cats

1 In the Middle Ages, people thought black cats were evil because they were witches in disguise.

2 In Britain, it's good luck if a black cat crosses your path and bad luck if it's a white cat. In North America, it's the other way round.

3 In olden times, sailors always took a cat on voyages. They reckoned cats were lucky because they killed rats and could tell if a storm was coming.

4 The Romans believed that if you dreamt you'd been scratched by a cat, you were in for a run of back luck.

5 Legend says cats were created on Noah's ark to keep the numbers of mice down. One of the lions on board sneezed a cat out of his nose.

Cats of books, stage and screen

Cats have also had starring roles in fairy tales, books, films, poems and musicals. Here are a few famous felines, for starters...

Puss in Boots

Puss in Boots is a French fairy tale by Charles Perrault. The story tells of a cunning cat who tricks a fierce ogre into turning into a mouse. The cat then eats the ogre and grabs his castle and riches for his master. Puss later helps his master win a princess as his wife.

The Lion King

The Lion King is a film set in Africa and stars Simba, son of the lion king. His wicked uncle, Scar, kills the king then tries to blame Simba. Ashamed, Simba runs away and Scar grabs the throne. Later, Simba fights Scar and take his rightful place as king.

Cats

Cats, the musical, is based on a book of poems by T. S. Eliot, called *Old Possum's Book of Practical Cats*. It stars a whole cast of cats with unusual names – meet Old Deuteronomy, the Rum Tum Tugger, Jennyanydots, Macavity and many more.

Famous felines

Mrs Chippy

In 1914, a tabby cat called Mrs Chippy (he was a tom) sailed to Antarctica with explorer, Ernest Shackleton. He was so popular that when he fell overboard into the icy ocean, the crew turned the ship round and went back to rescue him. A brilliant mouser, he loved sharpening his claws on the roof of the sled dogs' kennels, which drove them mad!

Secret Agent Fred

Fred the tabby began life as just another stray in New York, USA. But he soon hit the headlines when he helped the New York Police Department solve a dastardly crime. In 2006, fearless Fred went undercover, posing as a sick pet to catch a man pretending to be a vet. Fred won several medals for his bravery.

Station Master Tama

Tama, a stray cat at Kishi Station in Japan, rose to fame when she was officially named station master in 2007. Her main duty was to greet passengers as they got off the train. Tama was also given her own office – a converted ticket booth with a comfy bed, food, water and a litter tray.

Top cats

Simon

Simon the cat is the only feline to win the PDSA's Dickin medal, which is awarded to animals that have shown extraordinary bravery. Simon was the ship's cat on HMS *Amethyst*. When it came under fire in 1949 in the Yangtze river and was held captive for 101 days, Simon protected the ship's stores by hunting rats and also visited wounded sailors, cheering them up as they recovered.

Pyro the Kitten

Pyro the kitten was a stray, adopted by the photographer Bob Bird during World War II. He flew with the photographer, tucked in his flying jacket. One day, when the plane frosted over and Mr Bird was in danger of getting frostbite, he tucked his hands inside his flying jacket and Pyro kept them warm.

Lifesavers

There are also several stories of cats who have saved their owners when they have been taken ill. In the United States, Bart the cat woke his owner when her son, Jose, had a seizure. Jose was taken to hospital and survived. In Britain, Charley the cat saved the life of her diabetic owner when she collapsed. Clever Charley woke the owner's husband by patting his face with her paws.

Therapy cats

Therapy cats visit people in care homes, hospitals and other settings. Their visits cheer up the residents. Not only are they good company, they also make people feel relaxed and happy!

Amazing cat tales

Some people say cats have nine lives because they seem to be able to get out of all sorts of scrapes. But is it just a saying? Read these real-life tales and decide for yourself.

Kitty in a crate

In May 2006, a female cat called Chairman Mao, arrived in England after a month at sea. She had travelled all the way from China in a crate of crockery. She'd been having a snooze in the crate when it was loaded on to a ship. This plucky puss survived by drinking drops of water. She seemed remarkably well after her ordeal but didn't like being left on her own.

Fearless feline

When an old building in New York, USA, caught fire in 1996, nobody knew that five tiny kittens were trapped inside ... except for their mother, Scarlett. She risked her life darting into the flames and pulling out her kittens, one by one. Brave Scarlett suffered terrible burns in the rescue but made a remarkable recovery, and she and her kittens soon found new homes.

Real-life cat rescue

A terrified tabby kitten had a lucky escape when a typhoon struck the Philippines in 2009. Stuck on a hot, tin roof, she had nothing to eat or drink for days. A team of workers from IFAW (International Fund for Animal Welfare) managed to catch her and take her to an animal shelter, along with more than 3,000 other animals they had rescued.

Marvellous moggies

Most cats are mixed-up moggies of no specific breed. They can be long-haired, short-haired, or somewhere in between. They come in lots of colours, such as tabby, tortoiseshell, ginger, white and black.

You can easily spot a tabby by its stripy coat and the dark 'M'-shaped mark on its forehead. Some tabbies have dark tiger stripes. Others have stripes and spots as well.

Did you know?

The name 'tabby' comes from a French word for a kind of stripy silk cloth.

Some cats, including tabbies, have white patches of fur and a mix of colours under the stripes.

Did you know?

It's a myth that all ginger tabbies are male – there are female ginger tabbies, too!

Four curious cats

Chilled-out cat

The Ragdoll is a cute, long-haired cat with cream fur and brown markings. This laid-back puss is so relaxed, it goes floppy like a ragdoll when it's picked up. Sadly, Ragdolls tend to inherit heart problems. They also need a lot of grooming.

Fur-less feline

A Sphynx cat has no hair, apart from some very fine fur on its face, ears, paws and tail. At first glance, it might seem that the Sphynx would be ideal for allergy sufferers, but did you know that most reactions are caused by cat saliva, not fur? This means people can be just as allergic to Sphynx cats as other breeds. Cats use their sensitive fur to get information about the world about them, so it's much kinder and more natural to choose a breed with hair.

A tale of no tail

Manx cats come from the Isle of Man in England. They're famous for having tiny tails or no tails at all, which can give them back problems. A cat with no tail is a rumpy. A cat with a tiny tail is a stumpy.

Really wild

Bengals originated as a cross between Asian Leopard cats and domestic cats, and have coats with leopard-like patterns. They are active and can be quite tricky as they are very territorial.

Top tip

Remember that pedigree cats can have health problems resulting from being bred for their looks. If you are thinking about getting a cat, research any problems associated with certain breeds. Don't rule out a mixed-breed rescue cat – they're wonderful, too, and often healthier!

Built to hunt

Cats are carnivores, which means they eat meat, but pet cats have owners to give them their meals. In the wild, it's a different story – cats have to find their own food. That's why their bodies are built for hunting, especially at night...

Mobile ears for sharp hearing

Large eyes for seeing well in dim light

Sharp teeth for killing prey and ripping off pieces of meat

Rough tongue for eating and grooming

Sharp, curved claws for climbing and gripping prey

Did you know?

Most cats pull their claws in to protect them from harm. Cheetahs can't do this – their claws are always out.

Sensitive whiskers for sensing prey in the dark and feeling their way through narrow spaces

Fur coat for warmth and camouflage

Long tail for balance

Cat co-ordination

Cats are awesome athletes. They have strong muscles and fast reflexes for running, jumping, climbing, escaping from trouble and stalking their prey.

Jumping...

A cat can jump five times its own height in one bound. It bends its strong back legs, arches its back and leaps into the air.

Climbing...

Cats use their sharp claws for climbing. Going up's the easy bit. Coming down can be trickier.

Falling...

Cats usually seem to land on their feet when they fall. This is because they are very agile and have an amazing sense of balance, which helps them to turn the right way up if they fall.

Balancing...

Cats can walk along very narrow ledges or branches without falling off. A cat uses its long tail to help it to balance.

Did you know?

Cats walk on their toes and the balls of their feet. They never put their heels on the ground.

Super senses

A cat uses its super senses, including sight, hearing, smell and touch, for finding food and staying out of danger. It can even see well in the dark.

How can cats see in the dark?

1 A cat can see about six times better in the dark than you can. This is because it has a special layer of cells in its eyes for picking up any scraps of light.

2 In the dark, a cat's pupils grow very big and round to let in as much light as possible. In bright light, they narrow to tiny slits so the cat is not dazzled.

Did you know?

A cat's eyes seem to glow in the dark.
This is because the special layers of cells
bounce light back like a mirror. Spooky!

The cat's whiskers

A cat's whiskers are long, stiff hairs all around its face. They're twice as thick as normal cat hairs, and they're super-sensitive and super-useful. By twitching its whiskers, a cat can pick up tiny wobbles in the air made by an object, like a juicy mouse. Then the cat knows how where to pounce. Cats also use their whiskers for feeling their way around.

Scratch 'n' sniff

Does your cat always have a good sniff at its food before tucking in? Cats have an incredibly strong sense of smell that is much more sensitive than ours. They use smell to sniff out food, mates, enemies and other cats' territories – tom cats mark their territories with wee.

Did you know?

Cats don't like the pong of citrus (oranges and lemons) or mint but some cats go potty for a plant called catmint, which is sometimes called 'catnip'. They may sniff it, rub their heads in it and roll around it in, purring like mad.

Cat chat

Obviously, cats can't speak 'human' but how well can you 'speak' cat?
A cat makes many different sounds. Here are a few of these cat calls and
what they mean.

The top 4 cat calls

1 Purring is usually a sign your cat's feeling happy. Even tiny kittens purr, especially when they're drinking milk. But sometimes cats purr if they're feeling nervous or are in pain.

2 Meowing can mean different things. A short meow might mean 'Hello'; a medium-pitched meow might mean your cat wants something, like food, attention or letting out. Lots of meows in a row might mean your cat's worried or excited.

(3) Hissing happens if your cat's seriously scared, for example, if it's been backed into a corner by a dog. Hissing is a warning. It means 'I'm really, really dangerous and if you don't back off, I'll attack!'

(4) Teeth chattering is something your cat might do if it spots a bird through the window. It knows the bird's a tasty meal but can't get at it. What it's actually doing is practising its special killing bite, as if it has already got it's jaws round the bird.

Body language

Cats don't just use their voices to communicate. If you want to know what your cat's really feeling, take a look at its body language.

The top 10 things your cat's trying to tell you

1 Arched back – about to attack. Leave well alone.

2 Rolling over – feeling relaxed in your company.

3 Flattened ears – scared or getting ready to defend itself.

4 Pricked ears – alert and listening out.

5 Tail held high – a greeting or the sign of a confident cat.

6 Twitching tail – irritated, excited or in hunting mood.

7 Fluffed-up fur – trying to look big and scary.

8 Head-butting – saying hello to another cat or to you.

9 Rubbing legs – marking you as its territory.

10 Paddling with the paws – happy and contented but mind those claws!

Seven cat myths

Here are just a few of the common misunderstandings about cats – if you want to make sure you have what it takes to be a top cat owner then you'd better make sure you know the truth.

(1) Cats are low-maintenance pets

False! They may not need walking, like dogs, but cats still need a lot of time and attention. They also need regular visits to the vet for check-ups as well as any issues that may crop up.

(2) Cats can be left alone if you go away

False! Your cat should be left in the care of a responsible adult, who can feed them and check they are well. Most cats prefer to stay in their own home. If this isn't possible, get a recommendation for a local cattery. Taking your cat's basket and toys from home will help your pet to settle.

(3) Older cats need a kitten around to keep them young

False! Introducing a new kitten to the home can be extremely stressful for a cat. If you want to have a pair of cats it is wise to choose two kittens who have been together since birth, or socialized from an early age. Some cats will never accept a new animal into their home. Ask your vet for advice if you are thinking of introducing a new pet.

(4) Cats don't mind if they are left at home all day

False! Cats love company and it can be very stressful for them to be left alone all day. Make sure that you can offer a cat the home and companionship he or she will need to be happy.

(5) Leftovers are fine for a cat

A cat needs a healthy diet, which is balanced and contains all the right vitamins and nutrients he or she needs to stay well. Cats should be given a suitable cat food, not scraps from your meal, which may contain foods that aren't suitable, or may even be dangerous for your pet.

(6) The best drink for a cat is cow's milk

False! Cow's milk can upset cats' tummies and make them very unwell. Always provide clean water for your cat and place it in a suitable bowl away from its food and litter tray.

(7) Your cat will amuse him or herself

False! Cats are bright animals and need lots of exercise and mental stimulation to keep them fit and well. Ensuring they have plenty of toys and that you spend time playing with them is all part of being a responsible owner.

Are you a top cat owner?

Cats can make brilliant pets but would you make a brilliant owner? Here are some questions to ask yourself if you're thinking of getting a cat.

1 Can you give it a good home?

2 Can you give it the right food and water every day?

3 Can you take it to the vet if it's ill and for regular health checks?

4 Can you play with it and keep it company?

5 Can you make sure it's looked after if you're away?

6 Can you care for it for the rest of its life?

Answers

To be a purr-fect cat owner, you need to answer **YES** to every question and many more besides. If you answered **NO** to any of them, think again about getting a cat, as they are a big responsibility and a long-term commitment.

Did you know?

It's official, having a cat is good for you. It can teach you how to look after another living thing – provided you have an adult who can help you – and it has been found that stroking a cat can make you feel happier and calmer, too.

Here, kitty, kitty

How do you pick your purr-fect pet? Do you want an adult cat or a kitten? An adult cat may be calmer and used to living in a house but some adult cats may need time and patience to befriend. A kitten is lots of fun but needs special care. Here are some things to look out for if you're choosing a cat or a kitten:

Did you know?

Kittens shouldn't leave their mother until they are weaned – which means they have stopped drinking her milk. This can be up to 13 weeks of age.

Ears: clean with no tiny black specks that could be mites

Eyes: clear and bright. The third eyelid shouldn't be showing

Mouth: clean white teeth and pink healthy gums

Nose: silky soft and slightly damp

Fur: smooth and shiny with no signs of fleas

Tummy: slightly round but not pot-bellied, a sign of worms

Legs: strong and sturdy

Bottom: dry and clean under the tail

Behaviour: friendly and playful

My rescue cat

The best place to find your cat or kitten is an animal-rescue centre. They're always looking for good, caring homes for their cats.

How do I adopt a cat?

1 Visit your local cat-rescue centre and talk to someone who works there.

2 You tell them about yourself and the sort of cat you're looking for. You also meet some of the cats they care for.

3 If the rescue centre feels that you and your family are able to meet a cat's needs, they will help to match you with a pet that suits your home and lifestyle.

4 Someone from the rescue centre may come to your house to check it is cat-friendly and to meet the people and any other pets that live there.

5 You take your cat home. You may have to make a donation to help the centre with the cost of caring for the cat while it was with them.

6 A few weeks later, a worker calls to check how your cat's settling in.

Did you know?

In 2012, the RSPCA rehomed more than 29,500 cats and kittens. Some were strays, abandoned or cruelly treated. Others couldn't be looked after by their owners any longer.

Cat care essentials

Before you finally collect your cat, you'll need to get a few things ready. There are certain bits of kit your cat needs to make it feel right at home.

The top 7 bits of kitty kit

1 Bed or basket filled with comfortable bedding: put this in a dry, clean, quiet place where your cat won't be disturbed.

2 Food and water bowls: wash these every day. Keep these well away from the litter tray and keep food and water dishes spaced apart from each other.

3 Litter tray and scoop: a plastic tray where your cat can go to the toilet and litter that he or she is used to.

4 Brush and comb: for keeping your cat's coat in top condition.

5 Scratching post: choose a sturdy post, tall enough for your cat to use at full stretch.

6 Toys: things like catnip mice, balls, boxes and paper bags with the handles removed.

7 Cat flap: fit this to an outside door so your cat can go out and explore.

Home, sweet home

At last, it's time to bring your new pet home. You can get special plastic carriers for carrying cats. Line it with newspaper and a towel in case your cat has a little accident. It's also a good idea to take a familiar-smelling blanket or item for your cat to travel with and to make him or her feel safe in their new home.

When you get home, take things gently. Keep your cat in one room for a few days so it can settle in. Make sure the room is safe and put the cat's bed, food and water bowls, and litter tray in it. Gradually, you can let your cat explore the rest of your house.

If you've got another cat or dog, let your new pet get to know it slowly. Don't leave them alone together. Make sure your cat has got several safe places to escape to if it feels scared.

Dinner time

Your cat needs a healthy diet. Feed it on dry or tinned cat food, carefully following the instructions on the packet or tin. There are special types of food for adult cats, older cats and kittens. You can buy cat food from pet shops, the vet's or the supermarket. Ask your vet what's best to feed your cat or kitten.

The 5 top tips for feeding time

1 Cats naturally eat small portions of food, so split your cat's daily ration into several small meals throughout the day, unless your vet advises otherwise.

2 Make sure your cat always has fresh, clean water to drink. Don't give it milk instead of water. Milk can upset your cat's tummy.

3 Wash your cat's food and water bowls every day.

4 Put your cat's food and water bowls well away from its litter tray and keep the food and water apart from each other, as cats prefer to drink away from where they eat.

5 It's important not to overfeed your cat. It may become overweight and unhealthy.

Did you know?

If you notice your cat eating grass, don't worry!
It's perfectly normal. Cats sometimes eat grass
to help them digest their food.

Outdoor or indoor cat?

Most cats like going outdoors to play, hunt and go to the toilet. Some cats can live indoors if you live in a flat or near a busy road, but not all cats are suited to an indoor lifestyle. You'll need to try extra hard to keep an indoor cat happy and healthy. Cats that are used to roaming outside should not be made to stay inside.

What does an indoor cat need?

- At least one litter tray per cat in a quiet place. Clean out the litter tray(s) every day.
- Plenty of space to roam about – don't keep the cat in one room.
- A scratching post for sharpening its claws.
- Safe hiding places, including somewhere high up where it can perch.
- A comfortable place to rest and sleep.
- Plenty of toys and activities so it doesn't get bored.
- Grass for chewing – you can grow some in a pot.
- Lots of extra attention from you when your pet wants it!
- A constant supply of fresh water.
- A diet suitable for indoor cats – ask your vet for more information on this.

Did you know?

Cats are naturally nosy so you'll need to cat-proof your home. For example, shut washing machines and oven doors, and put a guard around the fire. Don't leave anything lying around, like electrical wires or plastic bags, that a cat or kitten could chew or get caught in.

Clever cat training guide

Cats like to do their own thing, but they are fast learners. If you show them how to do something, they'll quickly get the hang of it.

Litter-tray training

1 Fill the tray with cat litter. You can buy this from pet shops and supermarkets, but make sure it's a type your cat has used before.

2 Put the tray in a quiet place, away from your cat's food, water and bed.

3 Praise your cat quietly and offer a tasty treat when you see him or her using the tray.

4 In time, your cat may prefer to go to the toilet outdoors, but should always have a litter tray indoors, just in case.

Cat-flap training

1 Prop the flap partly open (you can use a clothes' peg to do this).

2 Tempt your cat to go through with a tasty treat.

3 Do this again from the other side so your cat goes out and in.

4 Your cat will quickly learn to push the flap open with its head.

Did you know?

Always talk to your cat gently. Never shout at it,
even if it's not doing what you want it to do.
It won't understand you but might feel nervous and scared.

Picking up your cat

It's important to know how to handle your cat properly or you might hurt your pampered pet. Here's a guide to picking up puss.

The proper way to pick up a cat or kitten

1 Never pick up a cat that looks frightened.

2 It's best to let an adult to pick up a cat, or to have them on-hand to help when you do.

3 To pick up a cat, put one hand under its chest and the other around its back legs and lift slowly. This way, you're supporting all of the cat's weight and not putting too much strain on its body.

4 Hold your cat against your body, so they feel secure.

5 Younger children should sit on the floor to hold their cat or kitten, as this reduces the chances of their pet being dropped and injured.

6 If a cat has had enough of being held and tries to get down, always release them gently. Don't try to keep hold of a cat that's struggling, or they may get upset or frightened.

Top tip

Most cats love being stroked, especially under their chins and on the tops of their heads, but cats don't really enjoy long cuddles, so it's best to wait for your cat to come to you — they may choose to sit on your lap for a fuss, but never force them to spend time with you.

Playtime!

Cats love to play. But playing isn't just for fun – it's the way a cat learns to hunt. This is what's happening when you see a kitten chasing its own tail! It also stops cats getting bored. You can buy special cat toys or make up your own games...

The top 4 cat-tastic games

1 Ping-pong pat-a-cake: a ping-pong ball's perfect for your cat to pat about and chase.

2 Mouse fishing: tie a small, soft toy mouse to a string, then pull it along for your cat to chase.

3 Paper bag pounce: let your cat pounce on a paper bag or play hide-and-seek.

4 Fishing rod toys to pull along for your cat to chase – make sure you choose a toy without feathers at the end, as these could be dangerous if swallowed.

Box clever

Cats love cardboard boxes. Next time you get a shoebox or a medium size cardboard box, pop it in a corner for your cat to curl up in. Boxes are great for playing, too. Cut holes in the sides so your cat can climb in and out, or dangle string in through the holes for your cat to play with.

Did you know?

Cats love catnaps! They snooze for up to 18 hours a day. That means they spend two-thirds of their lives fast asleep. Sleep's vital for saving up energy, so be sure not to disturb your sleeping kitty.

Keep your cat safe

Although there are many lovely toys and everyday objects that a cat can happily play with, there are also many household items that you should be careful to keep away from your cat as they could make him or her very ill. Your vet can advise you in more detail.

Lilies are highly toxic to cats, it is best not to have them inside the house as pot plants or cut flowers, or in your garden. Other houseplants to keep away from cats include amaryllis, cyclamen, hyacinths and ferns. If you are buying plants or flowers, always check the labels – usually there will be a warning if they should be kept away from pets. If you're still not sure, ask a vet.

Onions, garlic and chives should also be kept away from your cat, as they can make them extremely unwell.

Some cleaning materials can make your cat unwell. Store all cleaning materials in a cat-proof place.

Household chemicals such as anti-freeze and decorating materials should always be stored away from pets and any spillages should be cleaned up straight away.

Always keep human medicines away from cats and kittens. Never give your cat treatments intended for humans, as they could make him or her very ill indeed.

If you suspect your cat has been poisoned, take them to a vet immediately. If you know what they have been in contact with, take the bottle or packaging with you as it will help your vet to treat your cat quickly.

Did you know?

Some spot-on flea treatments for dogs are poisonous to cats. Ask your vet for advice and only use recommended flea treatments that are made for cats.

Clean cats

Is your cat always washing itself?
Cats groom their fur with their teeth,
paws and rough tongues. If there's a
bit they can't reach, they lick a paw
and use it as a facecloth instead.

Cats are very clean, but
sometimes they need
a bit of help. Long-haired
cats need daily brushing to
keep their fur tangle-free.
Short-haired cats need
less frequent brushing to
keep their coats in good
condition.

If your cat stops grooming itself or its fur looks dull, it may mean it's ill or stressed. It is best to take the cat to the vet's to check if anything is wrong.

Did you know?

When a cat grooms itself, it can swallow some of the loose hair. This makes a clump of fur in its tummy, called a fur ball. Often the cat just sicks the fur ball up, without any problem, but if you are worried about your cat, ask your vet for advice.

Kitten to cat

Here's how your super-cute kitten grows up into a super-cool adult cat...

1 A new-born kitten is tiny and helpless. It can't see or hear. Its mum licks it to help keep the kitten clean.

2 The kitten uses smell and touch to find its way to its mum's teats where it begins drinking her milk. It snuggles up to its mum for warmth.

3 The kitten grows quickly, putting on weight every day. When it is about two weeks old, it's able to hear and its eyes open. A kitten's eyes are blue, at first.

4 About a week later, the kitten takes its first steps and starts exploring. It copies what its mum does – by about 5-6 weeks it will copy her using the litter tray.

5 As it gets older, the kitten starts playing with its brothers and sisters. They play at fighting each other to practise their hunting skills.

6 At four weeks old, the kitten starts eating solid food. It can also groom itself, without its mum's help.

7 When a kitten is fully weaned and socialized, usually between eight to 13 weeks – although it does vary from kitten to kitten – it is ready to leave its mum and be chosen as a pet. If you're unsure if a kitten is ready to leave its mum, ask a vet for advice.

Did you know?

There are usually about four or five kittens in a litter. But in 1870, a Burmese cat, called Tarawood Antigone, gave birth to a record-breaking 19!

8 At six months old, the kitten is a young cat. Its coat is thick and glossy. Its eyes are green, orange or yellow.

9 By the time it is a year old, the cat is an adult. Male cats usually grow bigger than female cats.

10 As it gets older, your cat still likes to play, but may be less active and need a special diet.

Did you know?

A cat's normal life-span is about 14 years, but they can
live longer. A female tabby cat from England called
Ma lived to the ripe old age of 34!

Ask a vet

Part of being a good cat owner is making sure your pet is healthy. Here are some questions you might want to ask your vet.

Q: How often do I need to take my cat to the vet?

A: As soon as you get your cat, go for a health check. Your cat will need check-ups every year after that. If your cat looks ill, injured or it is in pain, or his or her eating habits or behaviour change, take your pet to the vet immediately.

Q: What does neutering mean?

A: It's a simple operation that stops your cat having any kittens. It is a good idea to have this done because there are lots of unwanted kittens.

Q: I'm going on holiday. What shall I do with my cat?

A: Cats prefer to stay in their own home, so ask a responsible friend, neighbour or a recommended pet-sitter to feed your cat and check it is fit and well. If this isn't possible, use a recommended cattery. Take your cat's own bed and toys so it feels at home.

Q: Why does my cat need injections?
A: To stop it getting nasty diseases like cat flu. A kitten needs its first injection at nine weeks old and its second at 12 weeks. Then it needs a booster jab every year.

Q: How does microchipping work?
A: A microchip is a tiny chip as big as a grain of rice that fits under your cat's skin. It has a special code, which needs to be registered on a database with your name and address. If a cat is found, the vet can find out who it belongs to by scanning the microchip.

Q: Why does my cat need insurance?
A: Pet insurance is always a good idea. If your cat does fall ill, insurance can cover the cost of expensive treatment.

Q: Does my cat need dental care?
A: As with humans, keeping your cat's teeth in good condition is really important. If your cat isn't eating, or has bad breath, is dribbling, or their teeth look yellow, take them to your vet for treatment. Your vet will be able to show you how to care for your cat's teeth.

Common cat problems

If your cat seems unwell, or off their food, or you notice any other symptoms that concern you, always contact a vet as quickly as possible and get your cat checked over.

Q: How do I know if my cat's got fleas?

A: If your cat is scratching, check its fur for fleas. Your vet can prescribe a suitable treatment for cats. Never use treatments intended for dogs or other animals – they could be poisonous to your cat.

Q: What should I do if I think my cat has worms?

A: Worms, picked up from other animals or by being outside, can make your cat unwell, but it's not always easy to tell if your pet has them. Your vet can advise you on worm prevention and suitable treatments.

Q: I think my cat's been in a fight – what should I do?

A: If your cat has been in a fight, and has been bitten, see your vet to have their wounds treated so that they don't get infected. Common places for cats to be bitten include their head, forelegs and tail.

Q: My cat has stopped eating. What should I do?

A: If a cat starts to refuse food or drinks more or less than usual, this may be a sign that your pet is feeling unwell. See your vet straight away.

Q: I've found an injured cat, what should I do?

A: Do not approach the animal or try to touch it. Tell an adult straight away and call the RSPCA on 0300 1234 999 for advice. Do not attempt to feed or give water to an injured animal. If possible, try to contain the cat and keep it still, quiet and warm. The RSPCA may suggest you take the cat to a local vet for treatment, or they may be able to collect the cat so it can be treated.

Cats quiz

1. What is a group of pet cats called?
a) a pride
b) a flock
c) a clowder

2. Which of these cats can't roar?
a) tiger
b) Siamese
c) lion

3. How many pets cats are there in the UK?
a) 8 million
b) 600 million
c) 60 million

4. What did the ancient Egyptians do with dead cats?

a) threw them into the river

b) burned them

c) mummified them

5. Which explorer did Mrs Chippy travel with?

a) Ernest Shackleton

b) Captain Scott

c) Neil Armstrong

6. How well can cats see in the dark?

a) not as well as humans

b) six times better than humans

c) ten times better than humans

7. What does it mean when a cat flattens its ears?

a) it's scared and preparing to defend itself

b) it's happy and relaxed

c) it's hunting for mice

8. How long do cats sleep for?

a) up to 8 hours a day

b) up to 10 hours a day

c) up to 18 hours a day

9. Why do cats sometimes eat grass?

a) they are vegetarians

b) to help them digest their food

c) to help them see better

10. How old was the oldest cat?

a) 34

b) 24

c) 14

Answers

1. c) 2. b) 3. a) 4. c) 5. a) 6. b) 7. a) 8. c) 9. b) 10. a)

Cat trivia

Did you know some of these amazing facts about our feline friends?

1 A female cat is called a queen.

2 A male cat is called a tom.

3 There are around 8 million domestic cats in the UK.

4 Almost a fifth of UK households own a cat.

5 A cat's normal temperature is around 38-39°C – slightly warmer than a human's.

6 Cat has 32 muscles in its ear. A human only has 12.

7 Cats have 244 bones and 517 muscles in their bodies.

8 A cat has 30 teeth.

9 Cats have been the subject of many famous pieces of art, including 'A Musical Gathering of Cats' by Van Kessel, 'Geraniums and Cats' by Renoir and 'Cats in the Garden' by Mao Yi.

All about the RSPCA

The RSPCA, or Royal Society for the Prevention of Cruelty to Animals, was founded in 1824 in London. It was the first British animal welfare charity and was originally mostly concerned with the welfare of animals such as pit ponies that worked down in the coal mines. The charity also worked with the hundreds of thousands of animals that served in the military during the First and Second World Wars.

Since then, the RSPCA has worked tirelessly to improve the lives of millions of animals, including those kept as pets and farm animals. It has 170 branches around the country, where staff and volunteers care for the animals that come into the centres. Many are re-homed after they have been nursed back to health and enjoy happiness with their new owners.

By educating people about animal welfare, the RSPCA aims to make sure that all animals live healthy, happy lives and are treated with compassion and respect.

To find out more visit: **www.rspca.org.uk**

Index

Also available

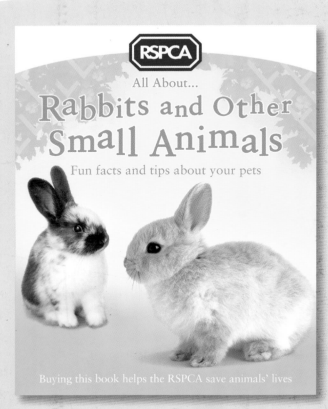